MADONNA AND CHILD

VIRGIN MARY AND THE BABY JESUS

COLORING BOOK

ASSEMBLED BY
MADDIE MAYFAIR

ISBN-13: 978-1522939375

ISBN-10: 1522939377

The Nativity by Israhel van Meckenem after Hans Holbein the Elder (circa 1490/1500).

Madonna and Child with an Angel by Annibale Carracci (1590/95).

The Rest on the Flight into Egypt by Simone Cantarini (17th Century).

The Adoration of the Shepherds by Annibale Carracci (1606).

The Virgin and Child on a Crescent with a Diadem by Albrecht Dürer (1514).

The Adoration of the Shepherds by Hendrik Goltzius (Style of Jacopo Bassano) (1594).

The Madonna on the Crescent by Albrecht Dürer (1510/11).

Suppliant Kneeling Before the Virgin and Child by Albrecht Altdorfer (circa 1519).

The Virgin Nursing the Child by Albrecht Dürer (1519).

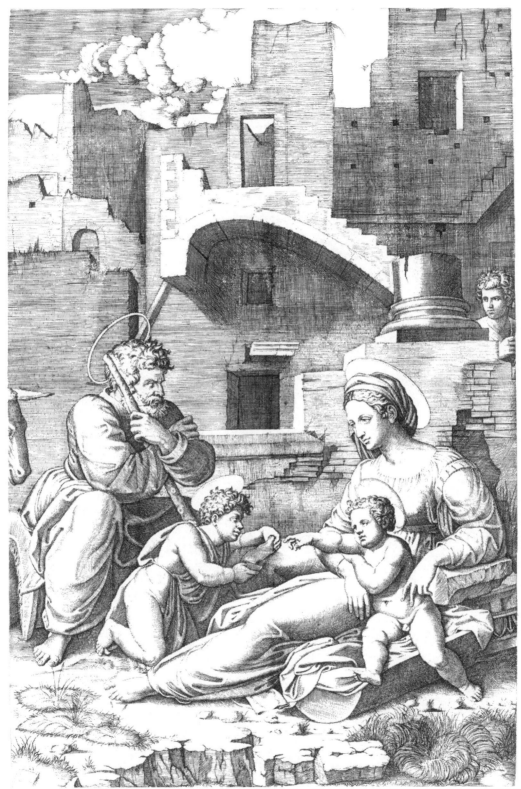

The Holy Family by Marcantonio Raimondi after Raphael (Italian, c. 1480 - c. 1534).

Virgin at the Window by Barthel Beham (German, 1502-1540).

The Virgin and Child by Giovanni Bottani (1725 – 1804).

The Glorification of the Virgin by Albrecht Durer (circa 1504).

Virgin and Child with Martyrs, after Pietro da Cortona (circa 1660).

Holy Family by Jacopo de' Barbari (1508/09).

The Nativity by Benedetto Montagna (circa 1507).

Lo. C. Petri Stephanoni Exc.

Madonna and Child with Angels by Lodovico Carracci (1595/1610).

The Adoration of the Magi after Lucas van Leyden (circa 1515).

The Holy Family with Saint Anne and Two Angels by Aegidius Sadeler II (circa 1593).

Madonna on a Crescent with the Dagger by Master N.H. (German, active first half 16th century)

Madonna on the Crescent Supported by Four Angels by Israhel van Meckenem (1490/1500).

Madonna in the Clouds by Federico Barocci (Italian, probably 1535 – 1612).

Madonna with Flower Vase by Barthel Beham (German 1502-1540).

Madonna on the Crescent by Martin Schongauer (circa 1470).

Madonna and Child by Hans Baldung Grien (1515/1517).

Madonna with a Parrot by Martin Schongauer (1470/75).

Madonna under a Palm Tree by Marcantonio Raimondi after Raphael (Italian, c. 1480 - c. 1534)

Enjoy even more *Colouring Books for Grown-Ups,* including:

Made in the USA
San Bernardino, CA
30 November 2016